P9-BIR-579

# Alfred's Kid's Guitar Course 1

## The Easiest Guitar Method Ever!

### Ron Manus • L.C. Harnsberger

Special thanks to our families, friends, and especially Kate Westin, Bruce Goldes, Ted Engelbart, everyone at Alfred, and Daisy Rock Guitars.

Cover and interior illustrations by Jeff Shelly. Interior photos by Karen Miller.

# Contents

**Selecting Your Guitar** . . . . . . . . . . . . . . . . . . . 3
  Steel Strings and Nylon Strings

**Acoustic Guitars and Electric Guitars** . . . . . . . 4
  Caring for Your Guitar

**Tuning Your Guitar** . . . . . . . . . . . . . . . . . . . . 5
  Tuning with the CD
  Tuning without the CD

**How to Hold Your Guitar** . . . . . . . . . . . . . . . 6

**Strumming the Strings** . . . . . . . . . . . . . . . . . 7
  Strumming with a Pick
  Strumming with Your Fingers
  *Time to Strum!*

**Strumming Notation** . . . . . . . . . . . . . . . . . . 8
  Beats
  The Quarter-Note Slash
  The Staff and Treble Clef
  Bar Lines, Measures, and Time Signatures
  *More Time to Strum*

**Using Your Left Hand** . . . . . . . . . . . . . . . . . 9
  Hand Position
  Placing a Finger on a String
  How to Read Chord Diagrams

**The Three-String C Chord** . . . . . . . . . . . . . . 10
  *My First Chord*

**The Quarter Rest** . . . . . . . . . . . . . . . . . . . . 11
  *Three Blind Mice*

**The Three-String G⁷ Chord** . . . . . . . . . . . . . 12
  *My Second Chord*

*Troubadour Song* . . . . . . . . . . . . . . . . . . . . . 13

*Skip to My Lou* . . . . . . . . . . . . . . . . . . . . . . . 14

*London Bridge* . . . . . . . . . . . . . . . . . . . . . . . 15

**The Three-String G Chord** . . . . . . . . . . . . . . 16
  *My Third Chord*

**Three Chords in One Song** . . . . . . . . . . . . . . 17
  *Rain Comes Down*

**The Repeat Sign** . . . . . . . . . . . . . . . . . . . . . 18
  *Merrily We Roll Along*

*Love Somebody* . . . . . . . . . . . . . . . . . . . . . . 19

**The Three-String D⁷ Chord** . . . . . . . . . . . . . 20
  *My Fourth Chord*

**Using D⁷ with Other Chords** . . . . . . . . . . . . 21

*When the Saints Go Marching In* . . . . . . . . . . 22

*Yankee Doodle* . . . . . . . . . . . . . . . . . . . . . . 23

**Getting Acquainted with Music Notation** . . . 24
  Notes
  The Staff
  The Music Alphabet
  Clefs
  The Quarter Note
  *Clap and Count out Loud*

**Notes on the First String: Introducing E** . . . . 26
  *Elizabeth, the Elephant*

**The Note E with Chords** . . . . . . . . . . . . . . . 27
  *Note and Strum*

**Notes on the First String: Introducing F** . . . . 28
  *Up-Down-Up*

**The Notes E and F with Chords** . . . . . . . . . . 29

**Notes on the First String: Introducing G** . . . . 30
  *The Mountain Climber*

**The Notes E, F, and G with Chords** . . . . . . . . 31
  *Brave in the Cave*

*Single Notes, Then Chord! Chord! Chord!* . . . . . . . 32

*Pumpkin Song* . . . . . . . . . . . . . . . . . . . . . . . 33

**Notes on the Second String: Introducing B** . . . 34
  *Two Open Strings*
  *Two-String Melody*

*Jumping Around* . . . . . . . . . . . . . . . . . . . . . 35

**Notes on the Second String: Introducing C** . . . 36
  *Ping Pong Song*
  *Soccer Game*

**The Half Rest** . . . . . . . . . . . . . . . . . . . . . . 37
  *When I Feel Best*

**Notes on the Second String: Introducing D** . . 38
  *A-Choo!*

**The Half Note** . . . . . . . . . . . . . . . . . . . . . . 39
  *Ode to Joy*

*Jingle Bells* . . . . . . . . . . . . . . . . . . . . . . . . . 40

*Mary Had a Little Lamb* . . . . . . . . . . . . . . . . 41

**Notes on the Third String: Introducing G** . . . . 42
  *Three Open Strings*
  *Little Steps and Big Leaps*

*Alouette* . . . . . . . . . . . . . . . . . . . . . . . . . . . 43

**Notes on the Third String: Introducing A** . . . . 44
  The Whole Note
  *A Is Easy!*
  *Taking a Walk*

*Aura Lee* . . . . . . . . . . . . . . . . . . . . . . . . . . . 45

*She'll Be Comin' 'Round the Mountain* . . . . . . . . . 46

**Music Matching Games** . . . . . . . . . . . . . . . . 47

**Diploma** . . . . . . . . . . . . . . . . . . . . . . . . . . 48

# Selecting Your Guitar

Guitars come in different types and sizes. It's important to choose a guitar that's just the right size for you, and not one that's too big.

TOO BIG!

Just right.

Guitars come in three basic sizes: 1/2 size, 3/4 size, and full size. You should look and feel comfortable holding your guitar, so it's a good idea to have your local music store's guitar specialist evaluate if your guitar is the right size.

If the 1/2 size guitar is still too big for you, a baritone ukulele can be used instead of a guitar to learn everything in Book 1 of this course.

Baritone uke    1/2 size    3/4 size    Full size

## Steel Strings and Nylon Strings

**Steel strings** are found on both acoustic and electric guitars. They have a bright and brassy sound.

**Nylon strings** are usually found on classical and flamenco guitars. They have a mellow, delicate sound. Nylon strings are often easier for beginners to play because they are easier on the fingers than steel strings.

3

# Acoustic Guitars and Electric Guitars

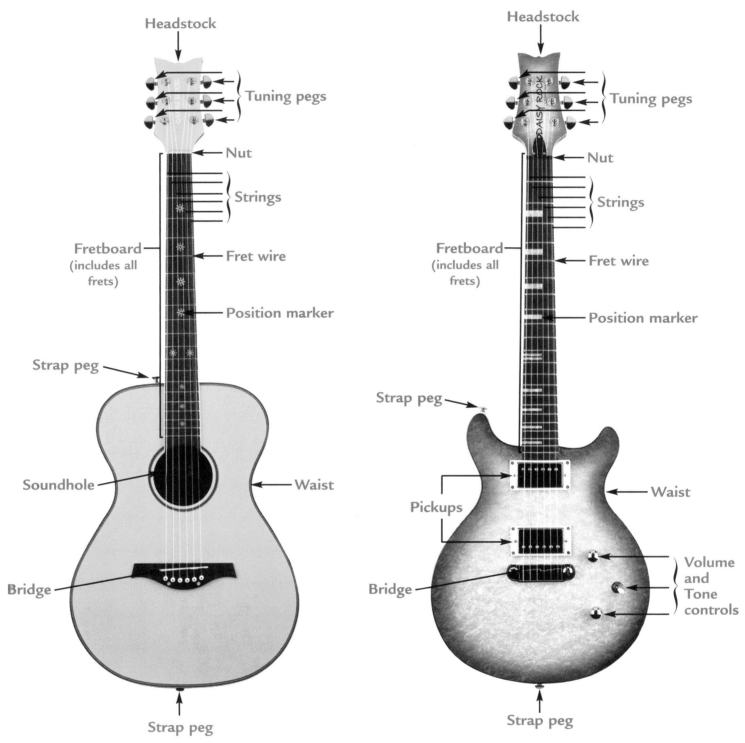

Headstock

Tuning pegs

Nut

Strings

Fretboard (includes all frets)

Fret wire

Position marker

Strap peg

Soundhole

Waist

Bridge

Strap peg

Headstock

Tuning pegs

Nut

Strings

Fretboard (includes all frets)

Fret wire

Position marker

Strap peg

Pickups

Waist

Bridge

Volume and Tone controls

Strap peg

## Caring for Your Guitar

Get to know your guitar and treat it like a friend. When you carry it, think of it as part of your body so you don't accidentally bump it against walls or furniture, and be especially sure not to drop it! Every time you're done playing, carefully dust off your guitar with a soft cloth, and be sure to put it away in its case.

# Tuning Your Guitar

First make sure your strings are wound properly around the tuning pegs. They should go from the inside to the outside, as in the picture. Some guitars have all six tuning pegs on the same side of the headstock, and in this case make sure all six strings are wound the same way, from inside out.

Turning a tuning peg clockwise makes the pitch lower. Turning a tuning peg counter-clockwise makes the pitch higher. Be sure not to tune the strings too high because they could break!

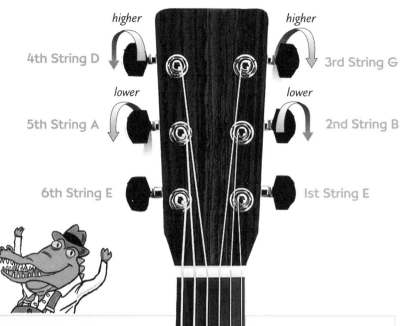

## Important:

Always remember that the thinnest, highest-sounding string, the one closest to the floor, is the first string. The thickest, lowest-sounding string, the one closest to the ceiling, is the sixth string. When guitarists say "the highest string," they mean the highest-sounding string.

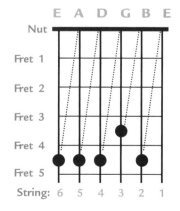

## Tuning with the CD  Tracks 1 & 2

### Using Your CD Player
Put the enhanced CD in your CD player and play Tracks 1 and 2. Listen to the directions and match each of your guitar's strings to its pitch on the CD.

### Using Your Computer
Put the enhanced CD in your computer's CD-ROM drive and click on "Tuning Your Guitar" in the table of contents. Follow the directions and listen carefully to get your guitar in tune.

## Tuning without the CD

### Tuning the Guitar to Itself
When your sixth string is in tune, you can tune the rest of the strings just using the guitar alone. First, tune the sixth string to E on the piano, then follow the instructions to the right to get the guitar in tune.

Press 5th fret of 6th string to get pitch of 5th string (A).

Press 5th fret of 5th string to get pitch of 4th string (D).

Press 5th fret of 4th string to get pitch of 3rd string (G).

Press 4th fret of 3rd string to get pitch of 2nd string (B).

Press 5th fret of 2nd string to get pitch of 1st string (E).

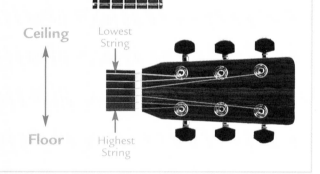

### Pitch Pipes and Electronic Tuners
If you don't have a piano available, buying an electronic tuner or pitch pipe is recommended. The salesperson at your music store can show you how to use them.

# How to Hold Your Guitar

Hold your guitar in the position that
is most comfortable for you.
Some positions are shown below.

**Standing with strap**

When you practice on your
own or want to play just for
fun, you might feel comfortable
sitting cross-legged on the floor
or on your bed. Just be sure to
keep good posture with your
back straight.

**Sitting on the floor**

# Strumming the Strings

To *strum* means to play the strings with your right hand by brushing quickly across them. There are two common ways of strumming the strings. One is with your fingers, and the other is with a pick.

## Strumming with a Pick

Hold the pick between your thumb and index finger. Hold it firmly, but don't squeeze it too hard.

Strum from the sixth string (the thickest, lowest-sounding string) to the first string (the thinnest, highest-sounding string).

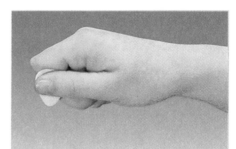

**Start near the top string.**

**Move mostly your wrist, not just your arm. Finish near the bottom string.**

## Strumming with Your Fingers

First decide if you feel more comfortable strumming with the side of your thumb or the nail of your index finger. The strumming motion is the same with the thumb or finger as it is when using the pick. Strum from the sixth string (the thickest, lowest-sounding string) to the first string (the thinnest, highest-sounding string).

**Strumming with the thumb**

**Strumming with the index finger**

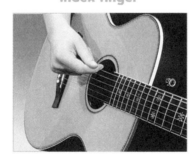

### Important:

Strum by mostly moving your wrist, not just your arm. Use as little motion as possible. Start as close to the top string as you can, and never let your hand move past the edge of the guitar.

## Time to Strum!  Track 3

Strum all six strings slowly and evenly.
Count your strums out loud as you play.
Repeat this exercise until you feel comfortable strumming the strings.

| strum | strum | strum | strum | strum | strum | strum | strum |
|---|---|---|---|---|---|---|---|
| / | / | / | / | / | / | / | / |
| Count: 1 | 2 | 3 | 4 | 5 | 6 | 7 | 8 |

# Strumming Notation

## Beats

Each strum you play is equal to one *beat*. Beats are even, like the ticking of a clock.

tick - tick - tick - tick
beat-beat-beat-beat

### Introducing the Quarter-Note slash

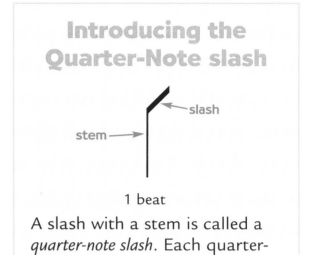

stem

slash

1 beat

A slash with a stem is called a *quarter-note slash*. Each quarter-note slash equals one beat.

## The Staff and Treble Clef

Guitar music is usually written on a five-line *staff* that has a *treble clef* at its beginning.

Treble clef

5
4
3
2
1

## Bar Lines, Measures, and Time Signatures

*Bar lines* divide the staff into equal parts called measures. A *double bar line* is used at the end to show you the music is finished.

Bar lines                    Double bar line

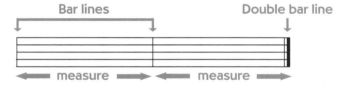

measure          measure

Measures are always filled with a certain number of beats. You know how many beats are in each measure by looking at the *time signature*, which is always at the beginning of the music. A $\frac{4}{4}$ time signature ("four-four time") means there are 4 equal beats in every measure.

Time signature

## More Time to Strum

Track 4

Play this example in $\frac{4}{4}$ time. It will sound the same as "Time to Strum," which you played on the previous page. Keep the beats even and count out loud.

**First time:** Strum all six strings as you did before.

Strum Strum Strum Strum    Strum Strum Strum Strum

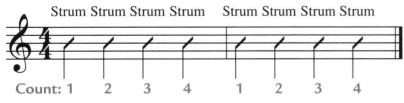

Count: 1    2    3    4       1    2    3    4

**Second time:** Strum starting with the third string, and strum only strings 3, 2, and 1.

Strumming strings 3–2–1

8

# Using Your Left Hand

## Hand Position

Learning to use your left-hand fingers easily starts with a good hand position. Place your hand so your thumb rests comfortably in the middle of the back of the neck. Position your fingers on the front of the neck as if you are gently squeezing a ball between them and your thumb. Keep your elbow in and your fingers curved.

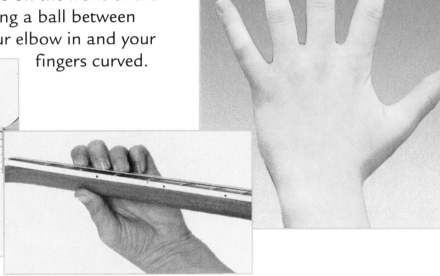

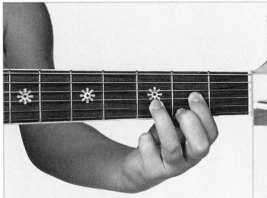

Keep elbow in and fingers curved

Like gently squeezing a ball between your fingertips and thumb

## Placing a Finger on a String

When you press a string with a left-hand finger, make sure you press firmly with the tip of your finger and as close to the fret wire as you can without actually being right on it. Short fingernails are important! This will create a clean, bright tone.

**RIGHT**
Finger presses the string down near the fret without actually being on it.

**WRONG**
Finger is too far from fret wire; tone is "buzzy" and indefinite.

**WRONG**
Finger is on top of fret wire; tone is muffled and unclear.

## How to Read Chord Diagrams

Chord diagrams show where to place your fingers. The example to the right shows finger 1 on the first string at the first fret. The Xs above the sixth, fifth and fourth strings tell you not to play them and only strum the third, second and first strings. Strings that are not played in a chord also look like dashed lines. The os above the second and third strings tell you these strings are to be played *open,* meaning without pressing down on them with a left-hand finger.

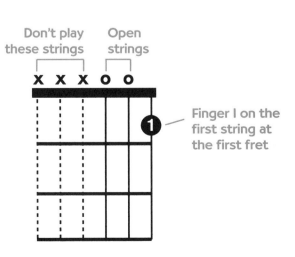

Don't play these strings

Open strings

X X X O O

Finger I on the first string at the first fret

9

# The Three-String C Chord

 Track 5

Use finger 1 to press the 2nd string at the 1st fret.
Strum strings 3–2–1.

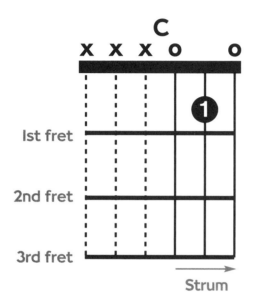

## Strumming

Strum the three-string C chord on each quarter-note slash ⌐. Make sure your strums are even. Count aloud as you play:

1–2–3–4 | 1–2–3–4.

Listen to the song on your CD to hear how it should sound!

# My First Chord Track 6

Remember: This means there are 4 beats in each measure.

| Count: | 1 | 2 | 3 | 4 | 1 | 2 | 3 | 4 |
|---|---|---|---|---|---|---|---|---|
| | Strum | Strum | Strum | the | Three | - String | C | Chord! |

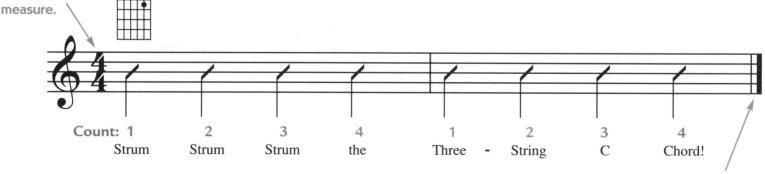

This **double bar line** tells us the music is finished.

# The Quarter Rest

### Introducing the Quarter Rest

1 beat

This strange-looking music symbol means to be silent for one beat. Stop the sound of the strings by lightly touching them with the side of your hand, as in the photo.

Track 7

### Rest Warm-up

Before playing "Three Blind Mice," practice this exercise until you are comfortable playing rests.

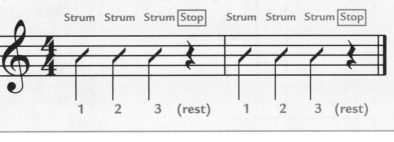

Strum  Strum  Strum  Stop    Strum  Strum  Strum  Stop

1    2    3    (rest)      1    2    3    (rest)

### Practice Tip

Strum the chords and have a friend sing the words.

# Three Blind Mice

Track 8   C

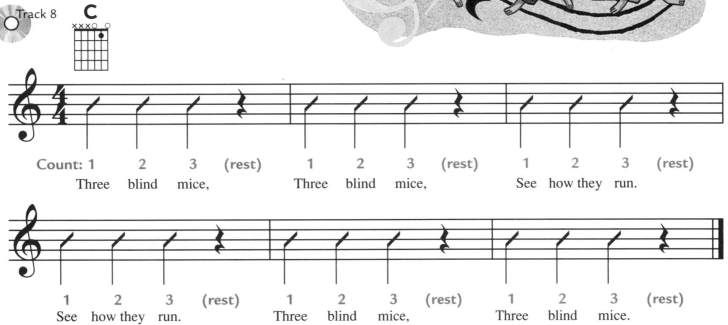

Count: 1    2    3    (rest)     1    2    3    (rest)     1    2    3    (rest)
Three  blind  mice,        Three  blind  mice,        See  how they  run.

1    2    3    (rest)     1    2    3    (rest)     1    2    3    (rest)
See  how they  run.        Three  blind  mice,        Three  blind  mice.

# The Three-String G⁷ Chord

Use finger 1 to press the 1st string at the 1st fret.
Strum strings 3–2–1.

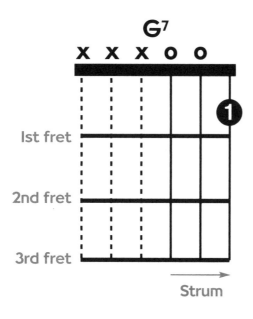

## My Second Chord

Track 10

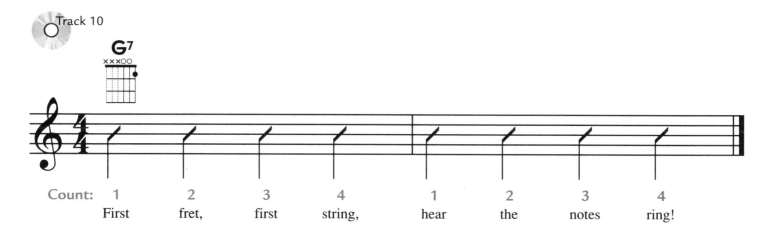

# Troubadour Song

Remember to stop the sound by lightly touching the strings with the side of your hand on each ♪. Wait one beat.

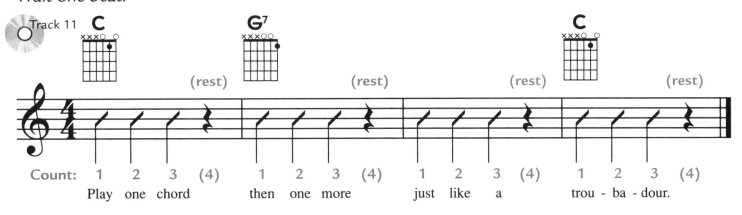

*A troubadour was a musician who traveled around singing and playing.

# Skip to My Lou

## Practice Tip

To change quickly from G⁷ to C in the last two measures, just move your finger from the 1st string to the 2nd string—that's not very far.

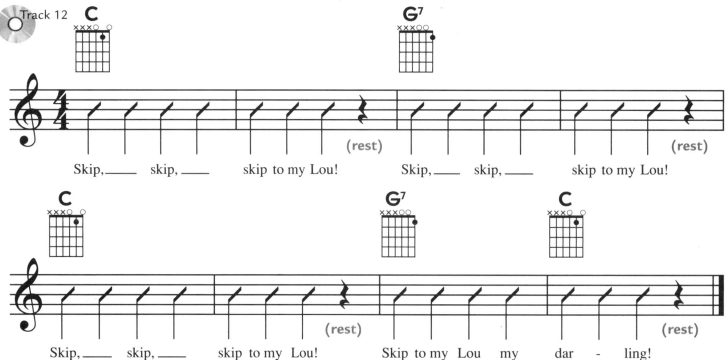

Track 12

Skip,____ skip,____ skip to my Lou! Skip,____ skip,____ skip to my Lou! (rest)

Skip,____ skip,____ skip to my Lou! Skip to my Lou my dar - ling! (rest)

# London Bridge

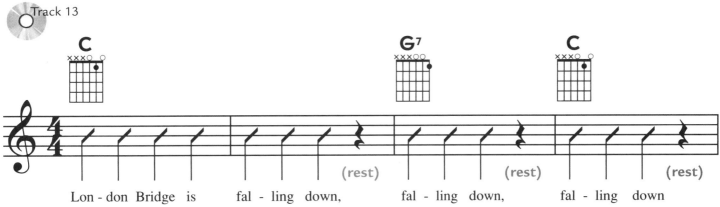

C                                          G⁷                    C

Lon - don Bridge is   fal - ling   down,   (rest)   fal - ling   down,   (rest)   fal - ling   down   (rest)

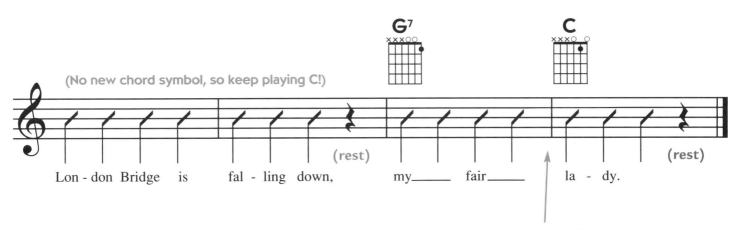

(No new chord symbol, so keep playing C!)          G⁷          C

Lon - don Bridge  is    fal - ling  down,   (rest)   my_____ fair_____   la - dy.   (rest)

Remember to move first finger
quickly back to the 2nd string to
play the C chord on the next beat.

15

# The Three-String G Chord

**Hear this chord!**
 Track 14

Use finger 3 to press the 1st string at the 3rd fret. Strum strings 3-2-1.

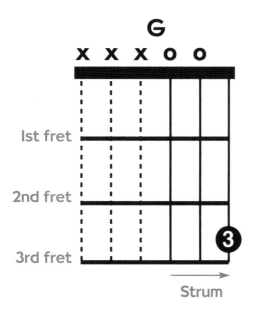

**G**

x x x o o

1st fret

2nd fret

3rd fret ③

Strum →

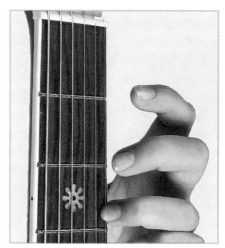

## My Third Chord

Track 15

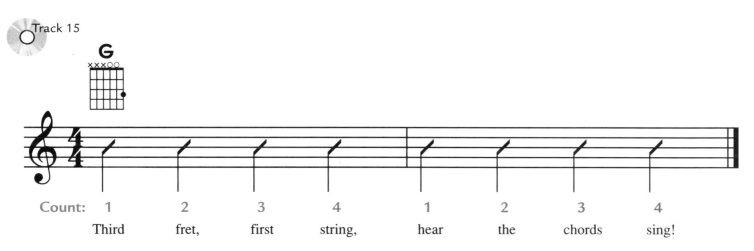

Count: 1   2   3   4   1   2   3   4

Third   fret,   first   string,   hear   the   chords   sing!

# Three Chords in One Song

C

G⁷

G
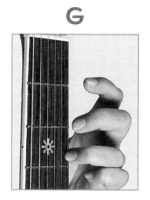

**Remember:**
This song has three different chords in it. At first, take your time and play slowly so that all the notes sound clearly. Don't forget to be silent for a beat on each quarter rest as you change to a new chord.

## Rain Comes Down

Track 16

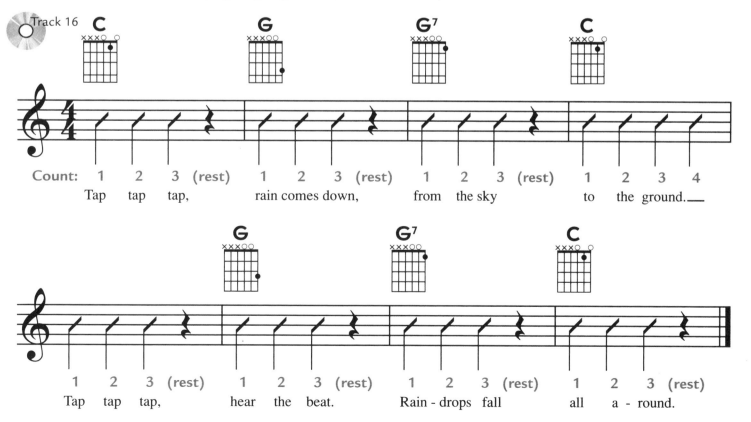

Count:  1    2    3  (rest)      1    2    3  (rest)      1    2    3  (rest)      1    2    3    4
         Tap  tap  tap,          rain comes down,          from  the  sky          to   the  ground. __

         1    2    3  (rest)      1    2    3  (rest)      1    2    3  (rest)      1    2    3  (rest)
         Tap  tap  tap,          hear  the  beat.          Rain-drops  fall         all  a - round.

17

# The Repeat Sign

## Introducing the Repeat Sign  :|

Double dots on the inside of a double bar line
mean to go back to the beginning and play again.

## Merrily We Roll Along

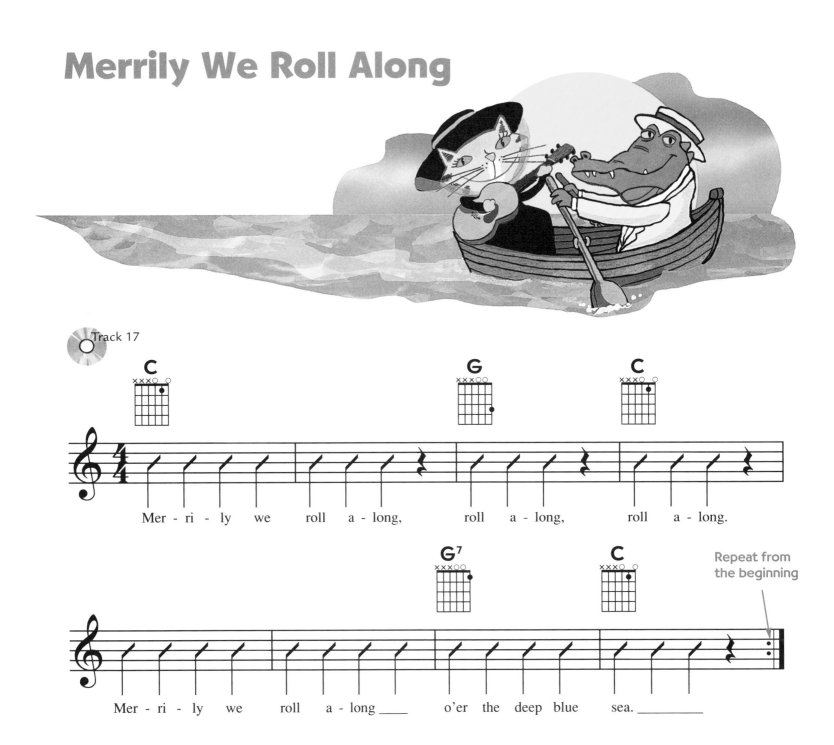

Track 17

C                                          G          C

Mer - ri - ly  we    roll  a - long,    roll  a - long,    roll  a - long.

G⁷        C                    Repeat from
                              the beginning

Mer - ri - ly  we    roll  a - long ____  o'er  the  deep  blue    sea. _____

18

# Love Somebody

# The Three-String D⁷ Chord

Use finger 1 to press the 2nd string at the
1st fret. Use fingers 2 and 3 to press the
3rd and 1st strings at the 2nd fret.
Strum strings 3–2–1.

**D⁷**

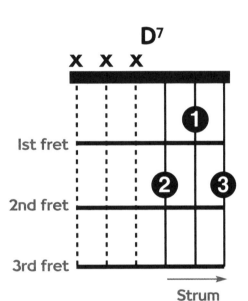

Strum

## My Fourth Chord

Track 20

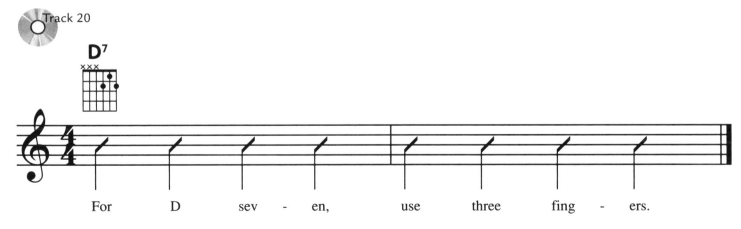

For    D    sev - en,    use    three    fing - ers.

20

# Using D⁷ with Other Chords

## Practice Tip

Before you play "When the Saints Go Marching In" and "Yankee Doodle," practice the exercises on this page. They will help you to change chords easily.

Play each exercise very slowly at first, and gradually play them faster. Don't move on to the songs until you can easily move from chord to chord without missing a beat.

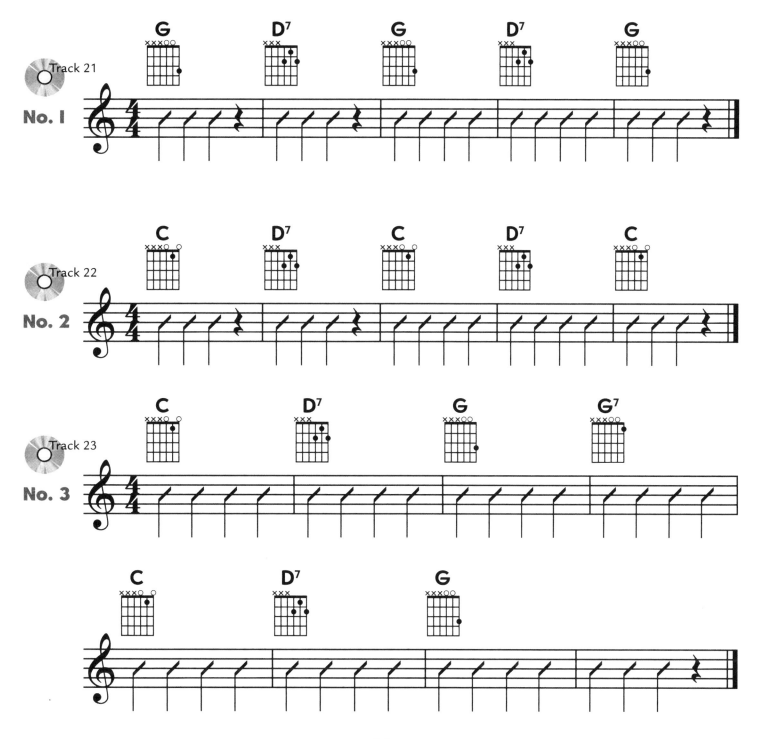

# When the Saints Go Marching In

Track 24

G

(rest) Oh when the saints ———————— go march-ing in, ——————

— Oh when the saints— go— march - ing— in, ——————

D⁷

G    G⁷    C

— Oh how I want———— to be— in that num - ber————

G    D⁷    G

——— When the saints— go— march - ing— in.———

22

# Yankee Doodle

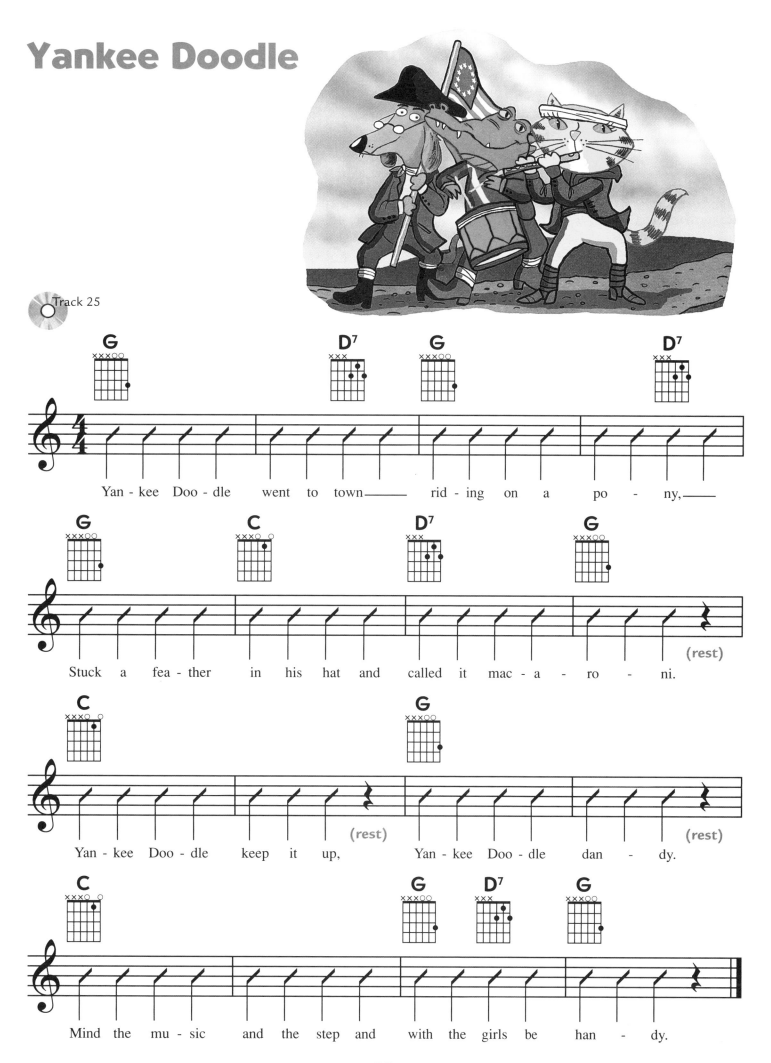

Track 25

**G**       **D⁷**   **G**       **D⁷**

Yan - kee Doo - dle went to town—— rid - ing on a po - ny,——

**G**       **C**       **D⁷**       **G**

Stuck a fea - ther in his hat and called it mac - a - ro - ni. (rest)

**C**            **G**

Yan - kee Doo - dle keep it up, (rest) Yan - kee Doo - dle dan - dy. (rest)

**C**       **G**   **D⁷**   **G**

Mind the mu - sic and the step and with the girls be han - dy.

# Getting Acquainted with Music Notation

## Notes

Musical sounds are represented by symbols called *notes*. Their time value is determined by their color (black or white), and by stems and flags attached to them.

## The Staff

Each note has a name. That name depends on where the note is found on the *staff*. The staff is made up of five horizontal lines and the spaces between those lines.

```
———————————— 5th LINE ————————————                    4th SPACE
———————— 4th LINE ————————                      3rd SPACE
———— 3rd LINE ————                      2nd SPACE
—— 2nd LINE ——                  1st SPACE
— 1st LINE ————
```

## The Music Alphabet

The notes are named after the first seven letters of the alphabet (A–G).

A    B    C    D    E    F    G

## Clefs

As music notation progressed through history, the staff had from two to twenty lines, and symbols were invented that would always give you a reference point for all the other notes. These symbols were called *clefs*.

Music for the guitar is written in the G or *treble clef*. Originally, the Gothic letter G was used on a four-line staff to show the pitch G.

This developed into the modern clef:

G

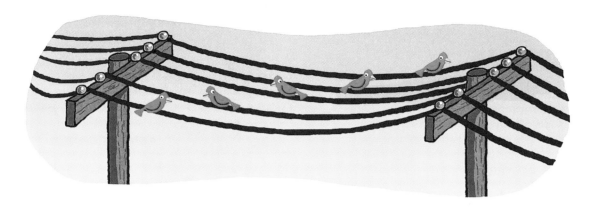

An easy way to remember the notes on the lines is using the phrase **E**very **G**ood **B**ird **D**oes **F**ly. Remembering the notes in the spaces is even easier because they spell the word **FACE**, which rhymes with "space."

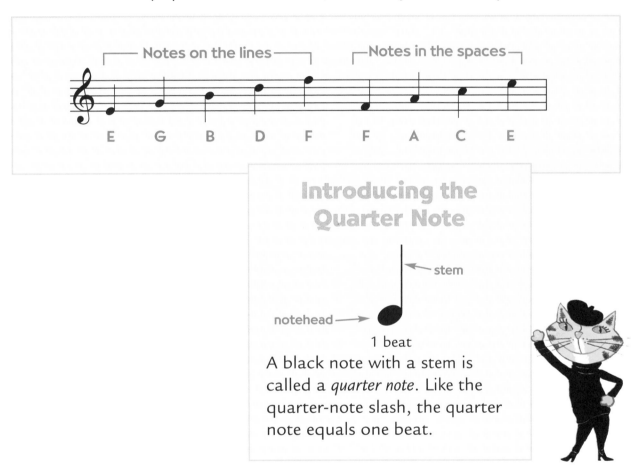

## Introducing the Quarter Note

stem

notehead →

1 beat

A black note with a stem is called a *quarter note*. Like the quarter-note slash, the quarter note equals one beat.

Track 26

# Clap and Count out Loud

# Notes on the First String
# Introducing E

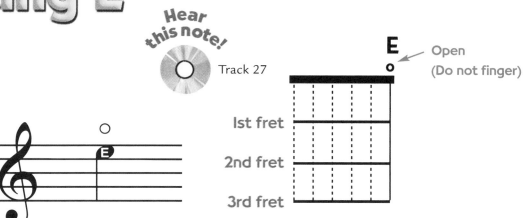

A note sitting on the top space of the treble clef staff is called E. To play this note, pick the *open* 1st string (meaning without putting a left-hand finger on it).

E — Open (Do not finger)

1st fret
2nd fret
3rd fret

# Elizabeth, the Elephant

## Picking

- Play each E slowly and evenly, using a *downpick* motion. We will use only downpicks for the rest of Book 1.
- Use only a little motion to pick each note, just like strumming.

Track 28

Count: 1 2 3 4   1 2 3 4   1 2 3 4   1 2 3 4

El - e - phants eat   en - chil - a - das,   es - pe - cial - ly   E - li - za - beth.

# The Note E with Chords

## Practice Tip

For this tune, notice that both the C and G⁷ chords are fingered with finger 1 at the first fret.

**C Chord**

**G⁷ Chord**

Simply move your finger over one string to change chords.

Track 29

## Note and Strum Warm-up

Before playing "Note and Strum" practice this exercise slowly until you are comfortable playing a note followed by a strum.

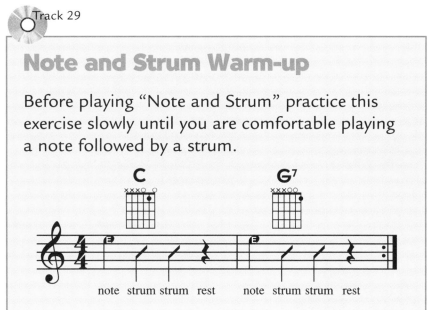

# Note and Strum

Track 30

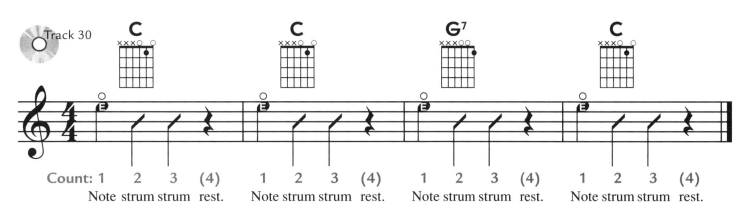

# Notes on the First String
## Introducing F

A note on the top line of the staff is called F. To play this note, use finger 1 to press the 1st string at the 1st fret. Use a down-pick motion to play only the 1st string.

**Hear this note!**
Track 31

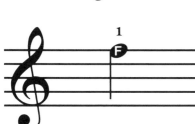

F

First finger

1st fret

2nd fret

3rd fret

Track 32

## Up-Down-Up Warm-up

Before playing "Up-Down-Up," practice this exercise until you are comfortable playing the note F.

## Up-Down-Up

Track 33

Start on E then up, first fin-ger. Down to E then up to the F.

28

# The Notes E and F with Chords

## Practice Tip

For this tune, notice that the note F and the G⁷ chord are both fingered with finger 1 at the 1st fret on the 1st string.

**Note F**

**G⁷ Chord**

Don't lift your 1st finger between the note F and the G⁷ chord.

Track 34

Hold down 1st finger

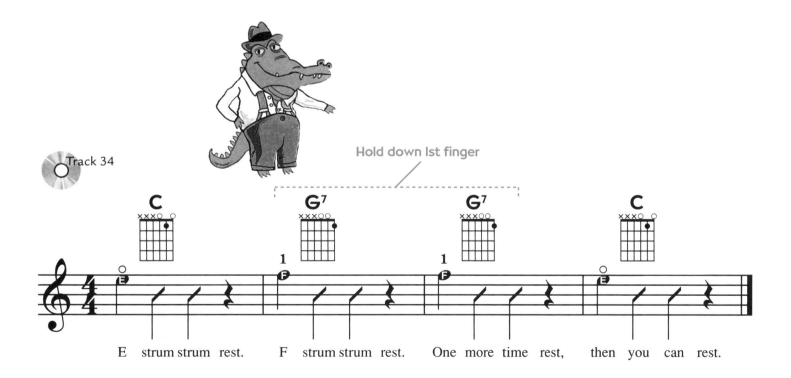

E    strum strum rest.    F    strum strum rest.    One more time rest,    then you can rest.

# Notes on the First String
# Introducing G

**Hear this note!**
Track 35

A note on the space above the staff is called G. Use finger 3 to press the 1st string at the 3rd fret. Use a downpick motion to play only the 1st string.

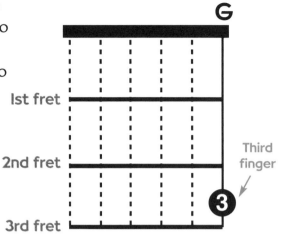

G

1st fret

2nd fret

3rd fret

Third finger

3

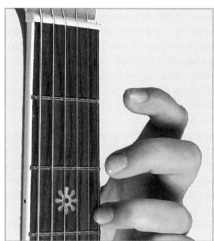

Track 36

## G Warm-up

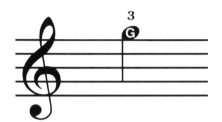

# The Mountain Climber

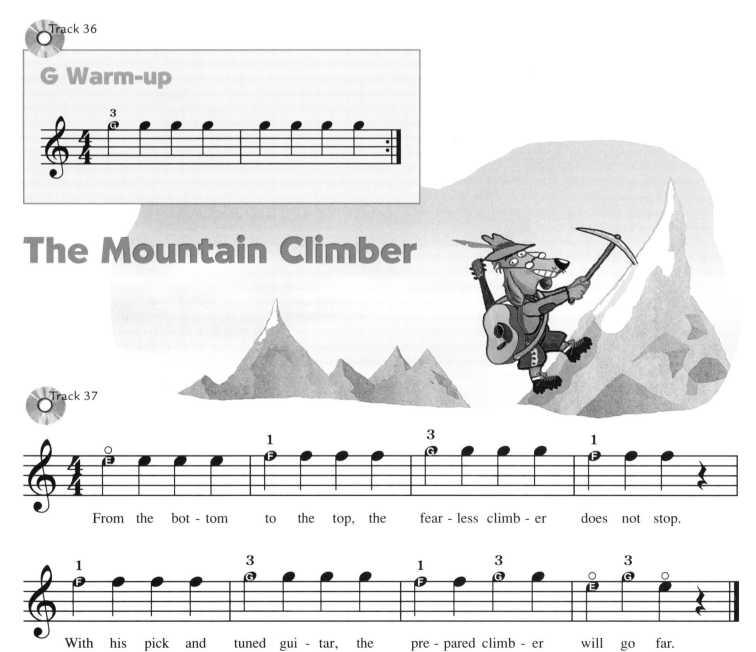

Track 37

From the bot - tom    to  the  top,  the    fear - less climb - er    does  not  stop.

With  his  pick  and    tuned gui - tar,  the    pre - pared climb - er    will  go  far.

30

# The Notes E, F, and G with Chords

## Practice Tip

Notice that the note G and the G chord are both fingered with finger 3 at the 3rd fret on the 1st string.

**Note G**

**G Chord**

Hold down the 3rd finger between the notes G and the G chord.

# Brave in the Cave

Track 38

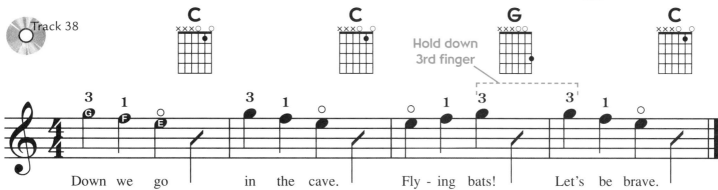

Down we go in the cave. Fly - ing bats! Let's be brave.

# Single Notes, Then Chord! Chord! Chord!

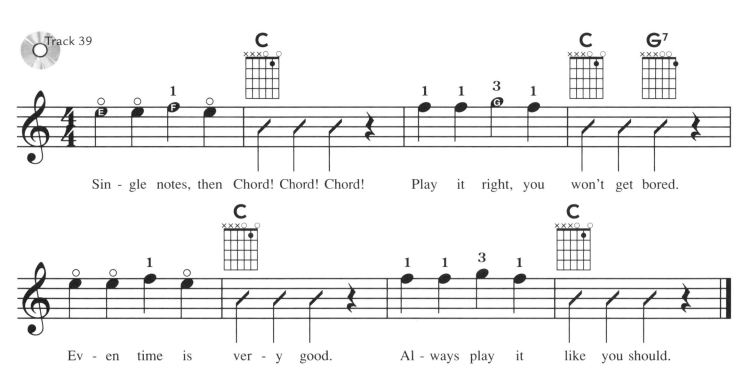

# Pumpkin Song

Track 40

G⁷

C

Can - dle  in  his  head.  Doesn't need  to  be  fed.

G⁷

C

Makes  a  tas - ty  pie.  Seeds help witch - es  fly!

# Notes on the Second String
# Introducing B

**Hear this note!** Track 41

A note on the middle line of the staff is called B. Play the 2nd string open.

B Open

1st fret

2nd fret

3rd fret

Track 42

## B Warm-up

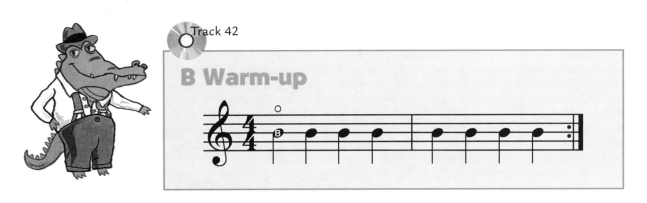

# Two Open Strings

Track 43

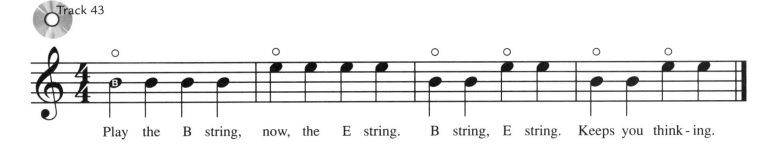

Play the B string, now, the E string. B string, E string. Keeps you think-ing.

# Two-String Melody

Track 44

Notes on two strings are fun to play. Notes on two strings, Oh! what fun!

# Jumping Around

Track 45

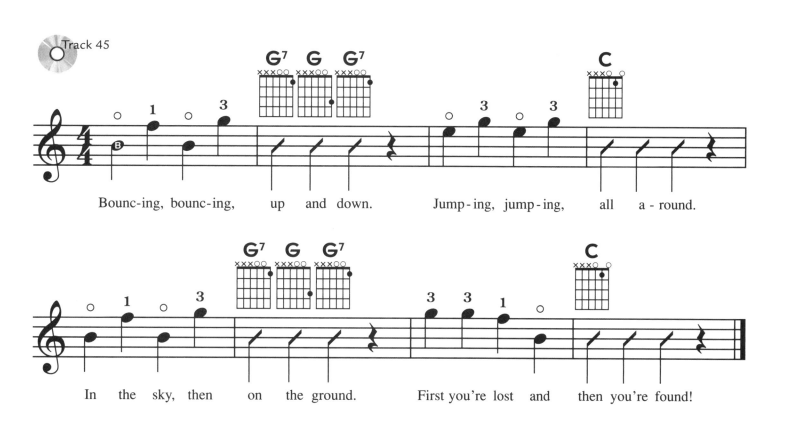

Bounc-ing, bounc-ing, up and down. Jump-ing, jump-ing, all a - round.

In the sky, then on the ground. First you're lost and then you're found!

35

# Notes on the Second String
## Introducing C

**Hear this note!**

Track 46

A note on the 3rd space of the staff is called C. Use finger 1 to press the 2nd string at the 1st fret. Pick only the 2nd string.

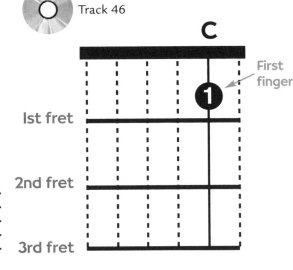

C

1st fret

2nd fret

3rd fret

First finger

Track 47

### C Warm-up

## Ping Pong Song

Track 48

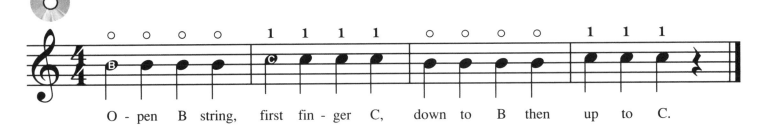

O - pen B string, first fin - ger C, down to B then up to C.

## Soccer Game

Track 49

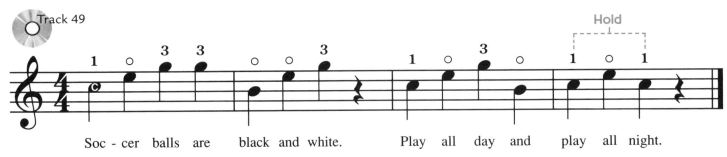

Hold

Soc - cer balls are black and white. Play all day and play all night.

36

# The Half Rest

## Introducing the Half Rest

This rest means do not play for two beats, which is the same as 𝄾 𝄾.

Track 50

**Clap and Count out Loud**

$\frac{4}{4}$ ♩ ♩ ♩ ♩ | ♩ ♩ − | ♩ 𝄾 ♩ 𝄾 | − | ♩ ♩ ‖

                                   (rest)(rest)     (rest)    (rest) (rest)(rest)

   1  2  3  4     1  2  (3) (4)   1  (2)  3  (4)   (1)  (2)  3  4

## Practice Tip

Notice that the note C and the D⁷ chord are both fingered with finger 1 at the 1st fret on the 2nd string.

In "When I Feel Best," hold the 1st finger down from the third beat of the 1st measure until the last beat of the 5th measure.

**Note C**

**D⁷ Chord**

# When I Feel Best

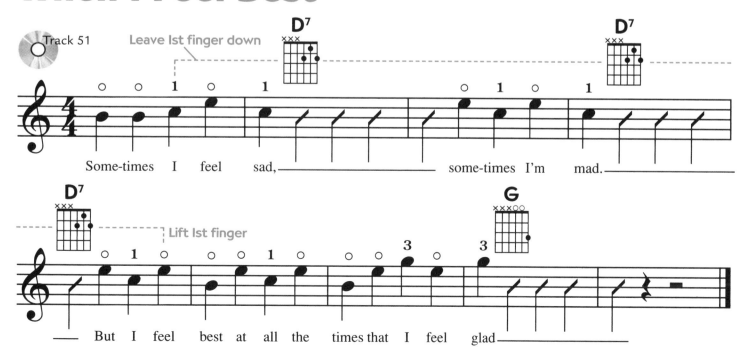

# Notes on the Second String
# Introducing D

Track 52

A note on the 4th line of the staff is called D. Use finger 3 to press the 2nd string at the 3rd fret. Pick only the 2nd string.

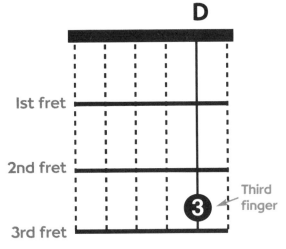

D

1st fret

2nd fret

3rd fret

3 ← Third finger

Track 53

## D Warm-up

## A-Choo!

Track 54

B and C and D are eas-y. Spil-ling pep-per makes me sneez-y.

"A-a-choo! A-a-choo!" Pep-per makes me go "A-choo!"

# The Half Note

## Introducing the Half Note

2 beats

This note lasts two beats.
It is twice as long as a quarter note.

Track 55

### Clap and Count out Loud

# Ode to Joy
Track 56

## from Beethoven's 9th Symphony

Ludwig van Beethoven

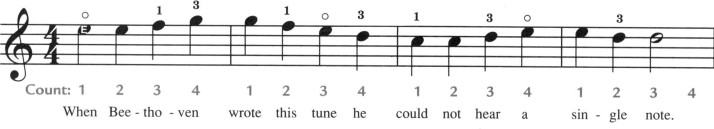

Count: 1 2 3 4 1 2 3 4 1 2 3 4 1 2 3 4

When Bee - tho - ven wrote this tune he could not hear a sin - gle note.

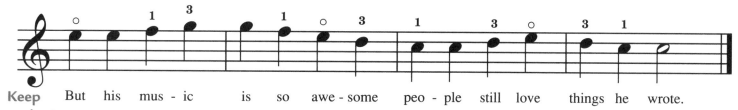

Keep
counting!

But his mus - ic is so awe - some peo - ple still love things he wrote.

# Jingle Bells

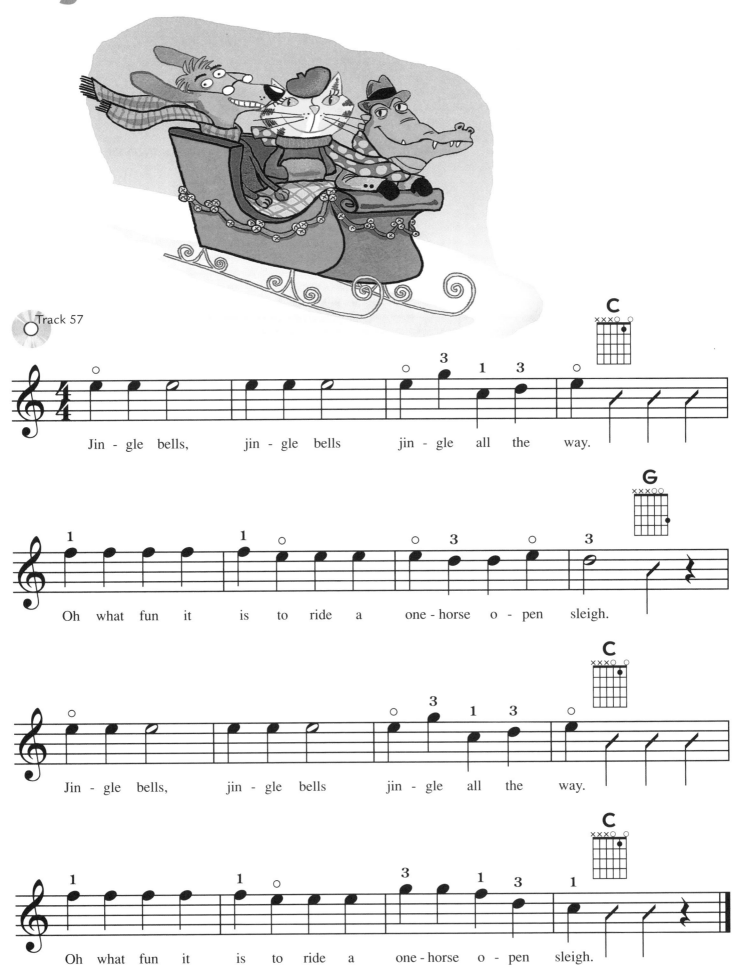

Track 57

Jin - gle bells, jin - gle bells jin - gle all the way.

Oh what fun it is to ride a one - horse o - pen sleigh.

Jin - gle bells, jin - gle bells jin - gle all the way.

Oh what fun it is to ride a one - horse o - pen sleigh.

# Mary Had a Little Lamb

Track 58

Ma - ry had a lit - tle lamb, lit - tle lamb, lit - tle lamb,

Ma - ry had a lit - tle lamb, its fleece was white as snow.

Ev - 'ry - where that Ma - ry went, Ma - ry went, Ma - ry went,

Ev - 'ry - where that Ma - ry went, the lamb was sure to go.

# Notes on the Third String
## Introducing G

Hear this note! Track 59

A note on the 2nd line of the staff is called G. Pick the 3rd string open.

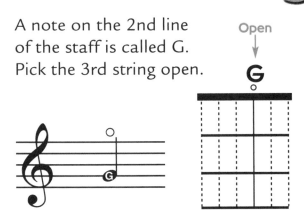

**G Warm-up**

Track 60

## Three Open Strings

Track 61

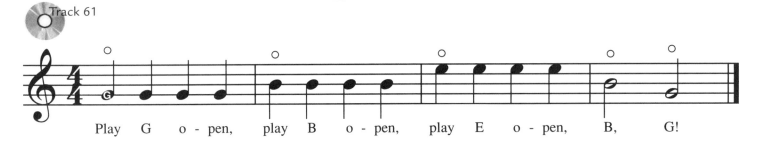

Play G o - pen, play B o - pen, play E o - pen, B, G!

## Little Steps and Big Leaps

Track 62

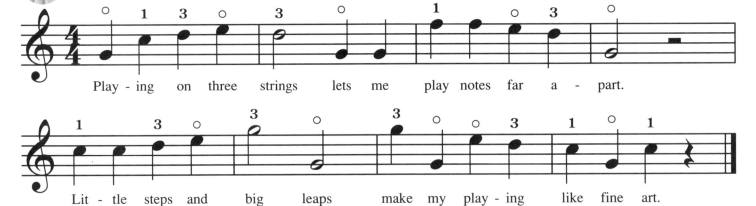

Play - ing on three strings lets me play notes far a - part.

Lit - tle steps and big leaps make my play - ing like fine art.

# Alouette

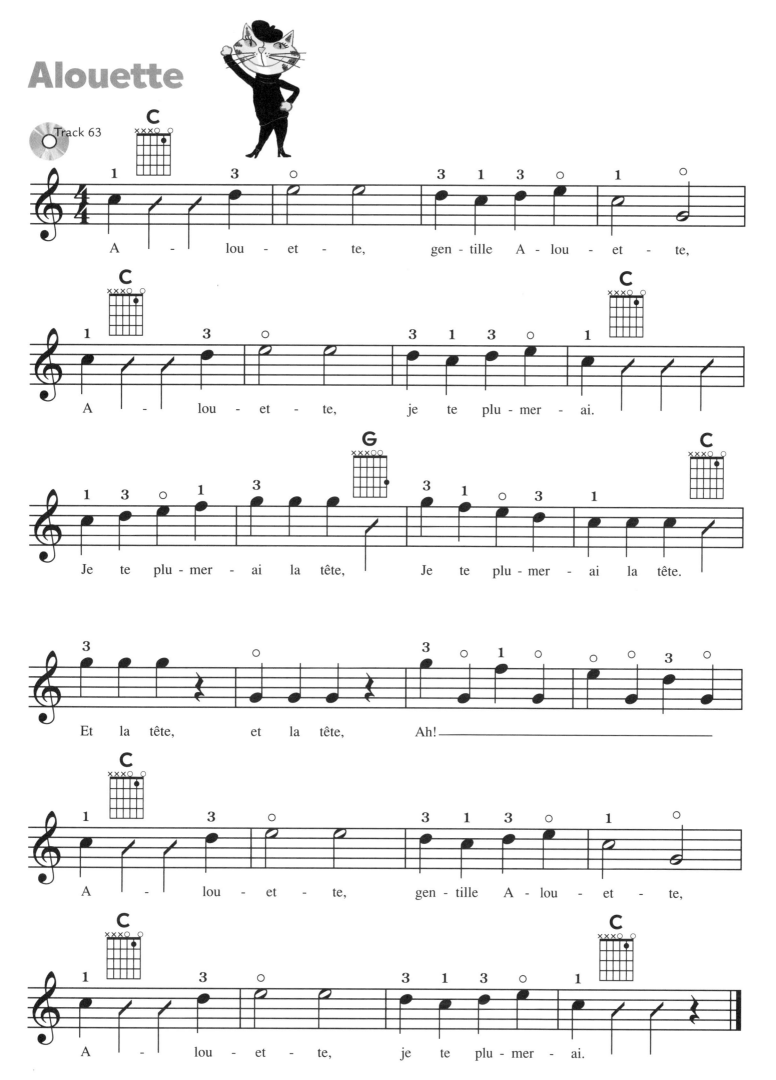

# Notes on the Third String
# Introducing A

A note on the 2nd space of the staff is called A. Use finger 2 to press the 3rd string at the 2nd fret. Pick only the third string.

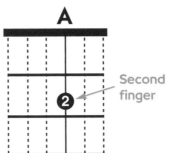

A

Second finger

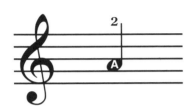

Track 65

## A Warm-up

**Introducing the Whole Note**

This note lasts four beats. It is as long as two half notes, or four quarter notes.

𝅝 4 beats

**Clap and Count out Loud**

Track 66

$\frac{4}{4}$ ♩ ♩ ♩ ♩ 𝅝 | 𝅗𝅥 ♩ ♩ 𝅝 ‖

1 2 3 4  1 2 3 4  1 2 3 4  1 2 3 4

## A Is Easy! Track 67

A is eas-y if you place your sec-ond fin-ger on the G string.

## Taking a Walk Track 68

Walk-ing up to D, then walk down to G.

D7                                    G

Then I add some chords         so I don't get bored.

# Aura Lee

Track 69

Elvis Presley recorded this folk song as a pop ballad called "Love Me Tender."

1. As the black-bird in the spring 'neath the wil-low tree,
2. sat and piped I heard him sing, sing of Au - ra Lee!

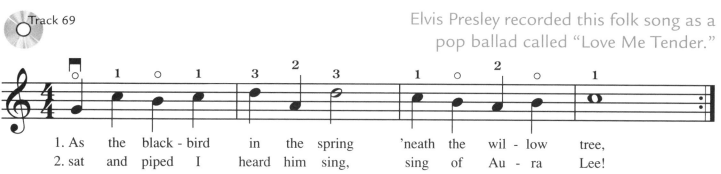

Au - ra Lee! Au - ra Lee! Maid of gold - en hair,

Sun - shine came a - long with thee and swal - lows in the air.

# She'll Be Comin' 'Round the Mountain

Track 70

# Music Matching Games

## Chords

Draw a line to match each chord frame on the left to the correct photo on the right.

1.

2.

3.

4.

## Symbols

Draw a line to match each symbol on the left to its name on the right.

1.         Treble clef

2.         Quarter note

3.         Whole note

4.         Quarter slash

5.         Half note

6.         Double bar line

7.         Half rest

8. 𝄾        Repeat sign

9.         Quarter rest

## Notes

Draw a line to match each note on the left to its correct music notation on the right.

1.

2.

3.

4.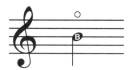

5.

6.

7.

8.

## Answer Key

**Chords**
1: page 10; 2: page 12; 3: page 16; 4: page 20

**Symbols**
1: page 44; 2: page 39; 3: page 25; 4: page 8;
5: page 25; 6: page 18; 7: page 37; 8: page 11;
9: page 8

**Notes**
1: page 26; 2: page 29; 3: page 30; 4: page 34;
5: page 36; 6: page 38; 7: page 42; 8: page 44

# Certificate of Promotion

### This certifies that

_____

has mastered and perfected
Book 1 of Alfred's Kid's Guitar Course
and is hereby promoted into
Book 2 of Alfred's Kid's Guitar Course

_____
Teacher / Parent

_____
Date